A DOG'S
LITTLE INSTRUCTION
BOOK

A DOG'S
LITTLE INSTRUCTION
BOOK

David Brawn

Thorsons
An Imprint of HarperCollins*Publishers*

Thorsons
An Imprint of HarperCollins*Publishers*
77-85 Fulham Palace Road,
Hammersmith, London W6 8JB

Published by Thorsons 1994
5 7 9 10 8 6 4

© David Brawn 1994

David Brawn asserts the moral right to
be identified as the author of this work

Illustrations by Wendy Jones
Design by Jo Ridgeway

A catalogue record for this book
is available from the British Library

ISBN 0 7225 2981 3

Printed in Great Britain by
HarperCollinsManufacturing Glasgow

Author's Note

Do not let your dog read this book. Instinct will have equipped him with most of its contents, and it is probably wise not to teach him any of the remaining pieces of advice which, through selective breeding, it has taken mankind centuries to remove.

You have been warned.

In memory of Sam
– there's no one quite like your first dog

🐾 Treat teddy bears with the contempt
they deserve

🐾 Learn to beg properly

🐾 Pretend you can't hear a silent dog whistle

- 🐾 Newspapers spread on the floor are not for reading

- 🐾 Don't eat vegetables—they give you wind

- 🐾 Never take a doggie chocolate in preference to the real thing

🐾 Stick a cold nose up a visitor's dress

🐾 Caged rodents are a snack waiting for the tin opener

🐾 Never eat your meal if you suspect it has a tablet in it

- Don't mess with hedgehogs

- Get to know your local police dog—you don't know when you'll need him

- Don't chase traffic

🐾 Prove to people you're not colour-blind

🐾 Sleep in a thoroughfare

🐾 Attack the vacuum cleaner, but be wary of the lawnmower

- Never use a dog loo

- Learn to pull chocolates off Christmas trees

- Leave nose marks on clean windows

- Be respectful towards corgis

- Never be seen in tartan

- Don't inhale talcum powder

- Don't let people blame you when *they* fart

- Don't attempt to crack open the tortoise

🐾 Don't countenance incest

🐾 Eat flies, but not wasps

🐾 Avoid fizzy drinks

🐾 Don't go to sleep on ants' nests

🐾 Hold a grudge against T.S.Eliot and Andrew Lloyd Webber

🐾 Pose for photographs, especially when you're not supposed to be in them

🐾 Howl at opera

🐾 Ask to be let out during a good film on TV

🐾 Pinch embarrassing rubbish from waste bins

- Be hygienic—don't lick yourself after licking someone's face

- Only swim in dirty water

- Watch sheepdog trials on television

- Don't eat a hot dog on principle

🐾 Get in the way

🐾 Drink from a birdbath in preference to a dog bowl

🐾 Chase squirrels

🐾 Never look behind a television set when a racing car drives off the screen

🐾 Bark at night

🐾 Never take 'no' for an answer

🐾 Avoid marking your territory on a prickly bush

🐾 Always do the sort of turds pooper scoopers are not designed to cope with

- Don't bite the hand that feeds you

- Bark in noise abatement areas

- Steer clear of broken glass

🐾 Accidentally walk on wet concrete

🐾 Never turn your back on a child with a water pistol

🐾 Clean between your toes

- Never get dressed up to appear on novelty postcards

- Leap on someone who's reading a large newspaper

- Learn to distinguish between your doorbell and one on the television

- Don't leave the table until you've been given something to eat

🐾 Don't be intimidated by larger breeds

🐾 Start a trend—yawn

🐾 Remember where you buried your bone

🐾 Ignore evolution and find a better way to greet other dogs

🐾 Don't crow about having private health insurance

Take the boredom out of long car journeys by:
   a) being sick
   b) barking at cyclists
   c) nose-printing on the windows

 Despise badger baiting

🐾   Be the leader of the pack

🐾   Live up to being 'man's best friend'

🐾   Hide in the undergrowth where humans
     fear to tread

🐾   Control your jealousy

🐾   Don't wet yourself when having your
     tummy tickled

🐾   When you get old, learn some new tricks

- ❧ Try being friendly with the neighbours' dog

- ❧ Wear your muzzle with pride

- ❧ Hide when it thunders

- ❧ Pick up as many grass seeds in your coat as you can

- Fight with the broom

- Beware the vet with the thermometer

- Play hide and seek

- Recognize when your owners are going on holiday

- Only chew squeaky toys in company

- Never play with a squeaky toy that's been de-squeaked

- Have phantom pregnancies

- Be a tug of war champion

- Don't let neutering turn you into a shy, retiring fattie

- Never eat manure, even if you've been told that it's good for you

🐾 Don't flash at the vicar

🐾 Don't steal food from dustbins

🐾 Take your vitamins

🐾 If it's hot, lie down in cold water

🐾 Don't be too possessive—it's unlikely that anyone *will* want to steal your bone

🐾 Use shampoo *and* conditioner

🐾 Don't bite your nails

- Don't take the blame for the cat's misdemeanors

- Only drag your bottom on plush carpet

- Always have an alibi

- Never chase a stuffed hare

- Don't pick a fight with a pit bull terrier (unless you are one)

- Ensure Father Christmas doesn't miss you out

- Bring comfort by visiting old people

🐾 Be someone's hero

🐾 Take your owners for walks

🐾 Learn to find your own way home

🐾 Learn to say sorry

- Don't eat off a plate someone might have licked

- Do Sphinx impressions

- Never forget your wolverine ancestry, even if you're a chihuahua

🐾 Aspire to be Top Dog

🐾 Don't chew chair and table legs

🐾 Push your nose under someone's elbow if you want attention

❧ Don't gnaw on chicken bones

❧ Never drink from a bowl with CAT on it

❧ Never trust someone who calls you 'dog' rather than by your name

🐾 If you live with another dog, don't rely on any leftover food still being there when you get back

🐾 Don't get depressed at Roadrunner

🐾 Take your master his slippers—don't chew them up

- Don't agree to an 'arranged marriage' unless you really like each other

- Have a large kennel, but resist ever going in it

🐾 Be brave

🐾 Keep your tail away from young children

🐾 Be inquisitive

🐾 Be a doggone nuisance

🐾 Go to obedience classes

🐾 Crap on the beach

- Refrain from cocking your leg up the Christmas tree

- Learn to recognize the word for 'dog' in five languages

🐾 Don't step on people's feet

🐾 Cultivate a sad expression

🐾 Children will love you if you play ball with them—until you puncture it

🐾 Don't eat hot food

🐾 Don't chew a biro

🐾 Don't take sides in domestic disputes

🐾 Get into bed on a Sunday morning

🐾 Don't snore

🐾 Be loyal and obedient—when it suits you

🐾 Be carried on escalators

❧ Look dejected when left outside shops and someone might give you something

❧ Make it as difficult as possible to be lifted onto the vet's table

- Don't be worried if your master shouts—his bark is worse than his bite

- Don't mistake an early dinner for a between-meal snack

🐾   Teach your offspring that puppies should be heard and not seen

🐾   Don't be a gundog if you hate:
   a) loud noises
   b) the outdoors
   c) the sight of blood

🐾 Don't be tempted to have a flutter on the greyhounds

🐾 Never underestimate the firepower of bad breath

🐾 Ponder over the origin of the phrase 'dog-eared'

🐾 No matter how revolting your meal, always ask for more

🐾 Pose by an old gramophone

🐾 Eat the sausage at retrieval classes

🐾 Don't bark at a dog in the mirror or you'll give yourself a nasty fright

🐾 Don't drink seawater

🐾 Shake any towels that are coming to dry you to ensure they're properly dead

🐾 Don't cock your leg up an electric fence

- Don't bark through a closed window at something that's too far away to hear it

- If you do have to take a bath, remember the soap is for shampooing, not eating

🐾 Don't tease a bigger dog for being tied up before checking he's not on an extending leash

🐾 Never eat slug pellets (or slugs)

🐾 Learn to snigger like Muttley

🐾 Always sleep on a freshly-made bed in preference to an unmade one

🐾 Know the sound of the fridge door

🐾 Get your vaccinations

🐾 Learn to unwrap your own presents

🐾 Stick your head out the window of a fast-moving car (or preferably the sunroof)

🐾 Don't chase sheep unless you're qualified

🐾 Find out where to buy Scooby Snacks

🐾 Stay indoors for fireworks

🐾 Don't let the arrival of a baby in the household lead to your being ignored

🐾 If you eat the carpet, make sure it's in a spot that can't easily be covered up

🐾 Smile

🐾 Fancy Lassie

🐾 When wet, don't shake until as many people as possible are within soaking distance

🐾 Don't eat grass – you'll make yourself sick

🐾 Wake a loved one with a lick

🐾 Only turn round and round before lying down if there's something there to flatten

🐾 Remember that playing with toilet paper is kids' stuff

🐾 Don't let on that you enjoyed it at the kennels

🐾 Make friends with the local butcher

🐾 Don't dig holes if you've nothing to put
in them

🐾 Learn to read 'No Dogs Allowed' signs—and ignore them

🐾 Don't be the underdog

🐾 Never fall over when cocking your leg

🐾 Don't walk to heel when you can be in front

🐾 Share your toys

🐾 Bark when strangers arrive at the house, not when they leave

- Remember, you're not a human being (who'd want to be?)

- Chase frisbees but not boomerangs

- Don't mate in public

🐾 If you want to be a successful gundog, don't eat the game

🐾 If you want to be a successful sheepdog, don't bite the sheep

🐾 Don't be humiliated—only enter a dog show if you have a chance of winning

🐾 Don't drink out of the toilet

🐾 Don't wolf down your food

- Only challenge a burglar if:
  a) he's obviously harmless
  b) he's stealing *you*

- Never take a tablet unless it's administered inside a Mars bar

🐾 Don't be selfish—share your fleas

🐾 Don't eat spiders

🐾 Wear a seat belt

🐾 Learn to shake hands

🐾 Wear your collar and tag

🐾 Prove your worth—don't be a dogsbody

- If you're a mongrel, lie about your parentage

- If you're a pedigree, deny any in-breeding

- Know the difference between a hosepipe and a snake—you might get wet

🐾 Refrain from wagging your tail near fine china

🐾 Relish a good brushing

🐾 Refute the idea that one year counts for seven
dog years once you get past ten

🐾 Despise anyone who says you talk to them

🐾 Know the sound of your master's car

🐾 If you train as a police dog, don't expect every criminal to have padded arms

🐾 Always let people know the phone is ringing, even if they have perfect hearing

🐾 If you want a lucky star, choose Sirius—the Dog Star

🐾 Don't get too worried if some drunk asks for 'the hair of the dog'

🐾 Be alert

🐾 Have a sixth sense

🐾 Keep your tail down when it's cold and windy

🐾 Ignore playmates who tell you you're beginning to look like your owner

🐾 Don't roll in dung

🐾 Don't 'fetch' when you can eat it there

🐾 Beware of passive smoking

🐾   Don't walk into furniture if you have to wear a surgical collar

🐾   If you become a sniffer dog, don't sniff too hard at the white powder

❧ Cock your head on one side to show you're listening

❧ Don't lie under the bird table and wonder why the birds don't come

🐾 Watch the sunset

🐾 Never *ever* be 'cute'

🐾 Look after your teeth

🐾 Never go to a pub without a garden

🐾 Don't whine

🐾 Don't lick your wounds

🐾 Don't eat toffees

🐾 Don't get fat

🐾 Know when it's unwise to push your luck

🐾 Rescue someone

🐾 Treat dogs that are half your size with
    indifference

🐾 See *Lady and the Tramp*

🐾 Know the difference between relaxation and lethargy—and practise both

🐾 Don't chase your tail

🐾 Watch fish in ornamental fish ponds—but don't fall in

🐾 Don't fall for the 'Walkies' ploy to get you to come for your bath

🐾 Don't walk under ladders

🐾 Don't steal liqueur chocolates if you suffer from hangovers

🐾 Know the sound of the ice cream van

🐾 If you hear someone say, 'I'll set the dog on you,' run and hide

🐾   Really clever dogs *don't* do tricks on command

🐾   Remember, today's playful kitten is tomorrow's fierce cat

🐾 Only agree to being a guard dog if you can stay awake at night

🐾 Always stand up in the back of cars to obscure the driver's rear view

- Avoid children's parties

- One man's scraps is a hungry dog's feast

- Never let anyone call you a mongrel

❧ Keep yourself clean—it's better than taking a bath

❧ Don't hang your head, unless it's just a ruse to get your own way

🐾 Lie in front of the fire, but not too close

🐾 Don't pee up a houseplant

🐾 Moult on dark carpets and car seats

🐾 Don't let your master take you for a walk as a cover for going out for a drink

🐾 Aspire to being the best of your breed, even if your owners are clearly not the best of theirs

🐾 Be proud of your private parts—don't be embarrassed about showing them off

🐾 Be nice to little boys—they'll grow up to be bigger than you

- Hide your tablet under your tongue for five minutes, then spit it out

- Lie somewhere warm when you're wet so you'll smell even stronger

- Learn to spell so you'll recognize 'W-A-L-K' and 'F-O-O-D'

- Never try to catch a ball that's small enough to swallow

❧ Don't easily be shifted from a comfy bed or chair without putting up a fight

❧ Don't try to mount the policeman's leg, even if uniforms do turn you on

- Eat snow, unless it's yellow

- Watch the tennis

- Never eat dogfood straight from the tin

🐾   Don't get frisky towards smelly feet

🐾   Ensure your owners boycott 'No Dogs' hotels

🐾   Wander off during a long 'stay'

🐾 Have a favourite armchair

🐾 Enjoy solar heating—sleep in the greenhouse

🐾 Own a 'Beware of the Dog' sign, regardless of temperament

- If someone tries to train you using the 'carrot and stick' method, eat the stick

- Never let a little rain dissuade you from taking a walk

🐾 Don't foul on the pavement unless it's next to a sign telling you not to

🐾 Remember, dogfood always looks meatier in the commercials

- Dissociate yourself from Pavlov

- Sulk

- Sleep in a particularly dark spot on the stairs

🐾 Never be fooled into mistaking a human pretending to bark for the real thing

🐾 Insist on commands directed at you being prefaced by 'Please'

- Only chew up *important* mail

- Require a minimum of 23 hours' rest a day

- Always take the shortest route

- See an analyst

🐾 Two of life's great mysteries are:
   a) If little boys do have puppy dogs' tails,
      have they been docked?
   b) If it's a dog's life, why is life a bitch?

🐾 Live in hope